ACKNOWLEDGEMENTS:

Nativity - *Four Quarters*
Beside the Wide River - *Painted Bride Quarterly*
Snow on the Boulevard - *Painted Bride Quarterly*
Not Even - *Painted Bride Quarterly*

ISBN: 9798441693509

HERE

(Muir Woods, to guard the guardians)
Listen,
here is a place to hear
the world whispering,
a place where the voice of a stream
becomes an oration,
where feathered boughs bend
to brush our hair and bless
the lightning in our skulls
that dims itself to flicker
beside the flash
of the planet's own pulse.
We press our minds against it
with kin rhythms in our hearts,
this place where the mantle parts
to heavy breast of sap and soil
and music.
The souls of rocks
and grey squirrels, of men
and ferns, of black deer,
and all that shines
are suckled here.
Listen,
A mother's head bows
to each baby brow.
A father genuflects
before every child.
Here
in the place of wild
where red wood guards
and holds in trust
eucalyptus and evergreen,
it can almost be seen
in rough rusty bark,
how earth blood is pulled
up to clouds, even to dark
empty space.
Sap and blood ascending
to head storms that settle
down to mist and rain of every dream
that ever hid in fur or wood

or skin or feather or stone
or word or air, listen,
the world breathes easy
here.

IF CHERRY BLOSSOMS CAN PRIMP

and preen along ponds and river banks,
and forsythia drapes its branches with sunlight,
and crocuses squeeze unwavering
into purples, whites and yellows, and
red bud trees begin their lavender blush,
and the daffodils wildly paint
warm! warm! all over the yard
in brash yellow letters and, right now,
my hummingbird makes his first visit
to dip into sweet entitlements,
then I trust in the hope
for more tomorrows.

SEASON THAT HUMS

Trees exploded
with buds not green
but almost yellow, chartreuse,
greedy to gobble
their light breakfast
of sun,

a crazy sun, beaming
like a lusty lunatic,
shooting up each May day
with bullets of gold,
ricochet, ricochet,
lawn to blossom to tree
and see,
birds are glowing.

Shading Spring is
a light thing. Sun pulses
swallowed or tossed back,
mixing waves into a vision.
Color understands itself
between a petal
and a smiling eye,

and birds are glowing,
every tone of singing spectrums,
they are jamming, so much
fluted bird jazz, tweet
improvisations, cardinal
razzmatazz. My ears grin.

SEASON TO TURN

Now,
as green leaves, fades,
I am feeling the blush,
the reddening, gilding. Leaves
must change as the planet
finishes each revolution
around its sun. The sun
that churns and boils
and too will finally spend itself,
but not for millennia hence.
The lifetime of a sun is almost endless
when compared to planetary orbit,
or seventy or eighty years,
approximating my ending time,
as I redden or grow deeply gold,
moving toward letting go
and falling.

BIRDS ON OCTOBER AIR

The gain of beating their wings
is the push against something,
there would be no flight
in vacuum. The strength
of eleven wingstrokes
allows for a glide.

There is no emptiness
in atmosphere. Three
black birds soar
high into sky,
stroking against what
doesn't obviously exist.

COLORING

Autumn in a saucy child,
makes crayola mountains
with waxy shades and sun blaze.
Her favorite crayons
are orange yellow red
chartreuse magenta and gold.

When she feels a nip in the air
her cheeks dimple and she pretends
a blush of heat, smudges fingerpaints
in flames of color
to dazzle us, then
runs to hide.

She drops and scatters
crepe paper leaves
until the sky furrows
into a chilly frown, blankets her
in a heavy white quilt.

She's tucked away to nap
behind the bank of a brook
that froze into a diamond band
around her October November
sweetly waving
hand.

Watch
a leaf fall,
an informal funeral,
this bouyant pall bearing
of one autumn leaf
to its ground.

Responding to rushes of air
like that girl's amber hair
how it lifts, lightens in sun,
gestures at sky and
falls.

Like the leaf,
as it rises, whirls
shines like a tossed coin, and
falls to the damp,
to the embrace
to earth.

NOT EVEN

We place our faces close
and I want to swim,
you are such warm water.
We laugh through glistening clumps
of fallen Autumn or
run races from the theatre
to the car.

The days shorten.
The way we shape our smiles
and the candles inside
make our flashlight eyes
seem seasonal.
They glimmer
like a feast day.

I ask you
Can we keep that moon
as a jack-o-lantern?
You reply
Not even in October.
Pumpkins are carved
with that purpose
and can't be kept either.

RECOGNITIONS

I can be more witch in Ireland
than in Pennsylvania. I hear that clearly
in their bright syllables, and I will stay,
or dream to, on this island
where a ring fort diverts
a runway, and reluctant ruins
stand in the mist at Cashel.

Nearby, the mountain misses the bite
that *the devil himself took one day
and spat at St. Patrick.* The devil
couldn't stomach the rock of Cashel,
where I stand in wind
while the guide lectures. Her cheeks
blotched the way fair skin does
in a chill. Her Irish lilt
makes each recitation a truth.

*These towers were designed for siege,
high doors of heavy barricaded oak, and walls
two foot thick. These large stones
were mortared with a mixture..
animal blood, hair, soil, sand
and crushed shells. This mortar
hardened in such a manner, it became
part of the stone itself.*

Three years ago, she continues over the wind,
*lightning broke the chapel wall. Here it lies,
broken, as you see, in the middle of a stone,
not at any seam.*

So these towers are seamless,
and I disappear,
into passageways, climbing
steep stony spirals, listen
for the whispered workings of priests
and princes, listen
for the snap of a warrior's bone, syncopal flutes,
the brush of velvet skirt along
implacable stone.
I press my ear to a seam,
hear the mortar hum,

as it must have murmured
through each castled night, while stones
made themselves solid. Some lives
bled and some were shorn
to hold this place as fortress.

Ireland recognizes me, Cashel
conspires with my daydreams. My blood,
hair and crushed dreams, steadily
harden
into something already gone.
I listen for familiar winds.

COLD

too wide to see the far shore
of the frozen lake, cold as bright
as the shine off the forever ice surface, cold
as desperate as starlight
on the snow-laden pines,
the snow-buried vineyard, cold
almost measured by how much
a liquid metal will shrink into itself
inside a glass tube, cold that is told
in plumes of breath and car exhaust, cold
exposing all combustions, cold
that cracks the soul
into its own dark memory of death,
cold that slows even dreams to a groaning,
cold that rushes reason back to hide
inside the flash of a synapse, cold so black
that light freezes in skies and threatens
a refusal of morning, cold that staggers the red
from beating hearts, stunning them lavender,
pink, pale, to nothing moving, no currents
in veins, currents down the valleys, cold
that freezes the miraculous heron over the pond,
suspended forever near unyielding pines
and cowering willows, cold that wraps
around even the mind of God, until
only in the bundled hopes of a fallen angel
is anything trying to glow, trying
doggedly to warm toward the beginnings
of a thaw.

PARKWAY

To a muddy, rutted lot
beside the little Lehigh River,
I carry my lavish needs because
there might be reason
in the water.
My unravelling reaches

like a hand into the flow
and it takes a framing shape
around my grabbing fingers.
It takes a moving shape, but
holds no shape, runs only
through. My eyes release

nothing, my throat swallows
against solid walls. I am weighted
here, held motionless and dry.
I contain this source too long,
forever, dammed to a depth
too dangerous to tap.

The water is facetted sunlight,
parallel shines over falls,
lace around rocks and branches,
smooth umber glass
between rapids. The water
Moves always, but stays
part of all of itself. When
my mind pulls back, wet
and empty, I see how an oak tree
splits, reaching different ways,
forming a V where
sinking day glares

across the little river. Lifts
a glittering wedge,
photographed, painted, described
in undulations. But motion will never
be carried away, it belongs
to its need to move.

TO FOG

There is a feeling to fog
against eyes, a way of knowing
atmosphere as plasma. This morning
the liquid air mutes the sky and
trees are indefinite, suggesting
their greens and disappearing
within a distance of steps.
The fog is shrinking perimeters
to a contained reality. I can't see
hills, fences, turns in the road, until
I begin the turning. This doesn't matter,

seeing too far ahead can be
overwhelming. Such fog, like
anesthesia pours over the morning,
recalibrating consciousness. Just as my gradual eyes
recognize deer, two doe, one small buck,
forming themselves near that wall
of assembling pines, a sudden
flashing of white tales
erases them all. But today
I am loving fog

when nothing is visible,
not the end of my walk,
not even my dog, loping
his usual scouting distance
ahead. Nothing is reported
back to me as I dream a world
forever a cloud and morning
snuggles tighter under my chin.
The deer evaporate, the pines fade and
finally, my dog comes back
grinning. He has been feasting
on magnified scents
and all that tantalizes
dogs. I too breath evergreen,
earth, and the not describable
fragrance of beginnings. Although
today is ordinary Spring, I wonder
how walks along the lost roads
of oblivion will be,

KATHLEEN MOSER

and whether, then,
my dog will report
anything
back to me.

FOG WEAVER

Tuesday is reluctant,
bunched at the chin of morning,
pulls a fog blanket over the lake,
snuggles under. I curl like the unborn,
wrapped in faded grey quilts,
knowing inside my spine
how beginnings require warmth,

that the fog over the lake
hides what I believe is still there.
Beyond the water's edge,
beginnings of docks,
there is more. Summer follows
Spring around mountain lakes.

Later, despite the chill
and Tuesday's hesitations, I wear a sweatshirt
over my robe, walk through my own haze
to the pale green dock.
I like the oldest chair, layers
of green rustoleum over layers
of rust and paint. Coffee fogs
over my cup, in front of my mouth.
Tuesday fogs against my eyes.

A rust-colored spider,
small as an eyelash,
works from a dock post to my leg,
back and forth, weaving needs.
It pulls silks from its body, twirling
and lacing me into domestic schemes.
Stitching fog to dock to Tuesday to me,
the spider is tireless, unaware
that one part of its foundations
wants to walk away for more coffee.

He hurries, post to leg to post.
My sighs drift across my empty cup. Sun steams
around the mountain top, Tuesday stretches, yawns,
hesitations
beginning to lift.

SPRUCE MUSIC

The music beneath spruce

winds around ivy vines,
where dew coated webs,
backlit by early sun,
are redwood bracelets,
and redwood sighs
tumble over themselves,
somersaulting with eucalyptus,
angels, other minor souls.

In the mind of its own time

this moment holds inself
beyond ink or inclinations,
seduction may be accomplished
in intentions;
the red deer near a white pine
can be convinced
to follow a forehead
to a clearing.

Only a moment loved enough

will be enfolded,
bound between linen,
memorized to novelty,
embossed onto bond,
like the music beneath spruce
that winds around ivy vines
with other minor souls.

willows try to be serious,
hold rainwater attitudes,
as all they must embrace
moves through them,
cloud scented winds,
traffic noises, loud
blue jay disagreements,
creek water slapping
over and against itself;

willows try to be patient,
adjust ribs and slivered leaves
in crinoline layers, seated
in their large demeanors,
earned when they rooted
with their own beginnings,
birthday circles and details
of wood, daily,
wrinkling into bark,

as if waiting clears the sky.

THE DAZZLE

The night sky at Promised Land State Park

I can't describe it, you've got to see...
David's hand squeezes mine as we
slip and shuffle though fallen leaves
down the steep path to lake edge.
He turns off the flashlight and both of us
close our eyes for a time, waiting,
allowing them to really open. *Look now!*

How we feel--younger than newborn,
smaller than innocence--beneath this midnight
arching over us like an endless inverted
black bowl, eleven millenia deep,
studded everywhere with that many stars,
as if smirking infinity needs to flaunt
her betrothal to chaos

in our faces--and with our open mouths
we have nothing to say while forever polishes
her galaxies, preening each curling nebula,
posing shamelessly above us--and there,
on the motionless surface of the lake
another night sky creates itself, identical
to the once over us, until the dazzle

of both skies roars
around us,
and the skies
in our eyes
grow strange
and bottomless.

THE STORM AND THE PREMONITION

Snow dances over snow, whirling
just above measurable depths,
white and horizontal, keening
across the chimney, an entire sky
becomes storm. Snow crowds
in ghost shapes over frozen alfalfa,
blows across the surface of what it is,
and all the snows before remain
exactly where they fell, weighted
beneath themselves, no longer
imagining flight. It's these white

aspirations I love to watch, mobs
of crystalline wishes in pirouettes,
delivering each other beyond the safest,
deepest drifts. These are snows
with no perimeters, suspended
by the violence of wind
between sky and ground
in gray violet air. The world
of these snows is a borderless place,
everything between can belong

in the pewter sky, sterling sky, stainless
steel sky, a realm of grays, a dreamed
and sixth dimension. This whirling world,
perceived through windows,
is how it will look when it is over.
How weightlessly I will dance
when I am formed of water crystals,
blown by collisions of pressure,
in waltzes with other ghosts,
other storm blown wraiths,
gathering in the white-out.

CHOOSING THE CHRISTMAS TREE

With so many garland boughs
each tree reaches in all directions
from its trunk and up to sky,
their scented oxygen breaths
exhaled into the forest air,
that is so sweetly filled
with the evergreen breathing
of Douglas fir and Fraser fir,
Concolor and Balsam fir,
white pine and hemlock,
and as his Daddy cuts
the chosen tree, little Gavin
gasps, inhaling the fragrant green,
everything breathing out and in,
sharing the blanket of gases
that wraps this living world
into a gift for eternity.

TRAIL TO MARCY DAM

Our snowshoes crunch
through the ice crust.
The powder beneath blows away
and I think of London's *White Fang*,
a dog sled in Klondike wilderness
crossing impossible drifts. Then,
I imagine members of the Donner Party,
the stronger ones, venturing outside
when the blizzard eased, hoping for game
finding nothing but winter. I remember Shivago
trudging the tundra, hallucinating his family,
chasing them down to finally stare
into the faces of frightened strangers.

We wear layers of silk and fleece,
down parkas, North Face windbreakers.
We are not in a classic novel, frontier tragedy
or epic movie. We walk confidently
over snow as if it were solid ground.
Hemlocks fringed with snow lace
bend over the trail, brushing our heads
and backpacks with snowy blessings.
Birches, their bark in strips, rise
from all the white like soldiers,
as if to enforce the peace of this mountain
in January, their Adirondack winter chapel,
where some of us faithful
frost the cold with prayers.

WIND CHILL

The cold
in the high peaks
is a predator. It stalks living things
sometimes so close, it takes my breath.
But I enter it willingly and bundled, though
my fingers ache and my cheeks burn.
The winds swirl snow into sparkles
around my steamy exhalations and
sunlight shines the icy snow
to diamonds. But I shiver still
as I push and glide, skiing as fast
as my muscles allow until
finally, puffing for air, I climb
the steeper parts of the trail
and my blood pumps harder
and hotter until, even my fingers
are warm. One more time,
I've outpaced
the cold.

ICE-FINGERED WORRIES

Midday, a steel-grey sky sneers overhead.
My toes ache. Billy jokes about warmer mittens
as we unpack lunches, huddle in the lean-to.
Carol offers me tea, *Warming from inside out
is best,* she smiles but I'm feeling worry. Ice needles
into my fingers holding my sandwich, I want
to start moving right away, to be warm again.
Let's start down now, I'm getting too cold.
Joe is surprised. *Already?* The others tease us.
She's right, I'm cold too, David agrees, knowing.
See you back at the lodge, and we start down

but no matter how hard we ski in cold like this,
it takes climbing before blood moves hard enough.
Finally almost two miles down pain fades, Skiing
is fun again. Back at the car I lift my water bottle
and find it's frozen solid. David hands me the one
kept warm in the car. Back in the lodge
a fire roars in the hearth, the main room noisy
as skiers and hikers all return. I'm settling in when
Carol and Josh suddenly decide, *Let's climb Mt. Joe,
one more short hike. I'm in!* David grins at me.
We won't be long. Carrying his snowshoes,
he kisses my cheek and follows them
outside into the cold that skulks around

the lodge and lake like a demon. As night falls
the outside thermometer creeps even lower. I watch
the clock while Chris speculates on tonight's menu,
others work the jigsaw puzzle, read their novels. Worry starts
dragging its nails along the back of my neck. Someone
mentions more snow in tomorrow's forecast. Worry
moves into my stomach, kicking a tantrum, pounds
across my forehead, pushes at my feet until
I begin to pace but worry follows me, is ahead
of me when I stop pacing, just daring me
to try to sit and then, *There they are, they're back!*
Josh comes in first, then David and Carol,
brushing off snow. I exhale slowly. All skiers
and hikers in the lodge now, safe and indoors.
The dark and cold sealing us in.

SHUSH

Whisper frost into December,
whisper in between
to me or to Houdini,
under the ice,
breathing whispers, breathing
crystal.

Houdini puts his mouth to edges
and breathes the spaces
between ice and water.
Whisper to me,
trying not to drown
or not to listen.

We both look up,
through pouring air,
to the luminous green
cold that closes
over this dream.

There must be a hole
in green,
the place where,
bending to hear whispers,
I fell.

Houdini fell in

to prove he could escape
within a whisper.
I fell
because
a whisper fell
first.

My face crystallizes,
my frosted fingers break.
Houdini makes an escape,
my cries weave a veil,
icy lace around my hair.

I make plans
to melt my face,
become magician,

escape even a dream.

SNOW ON THE BOULEVARD

Enough snow
to make everything snow.

We laughed snow.

Snow mounded into car shapes, porch shapes,
leveled into sidewalks, sparkled into streetlights.
Walking was pushing snow

along a city street,
for blocks and city blocks.
Our breath blew whirlpools
in falling snow.

I believed snow.

My eyelashes caught sky
till my snow-fringed vision
held the store
and the stone church
and the rows of porch railings
like crystal toys,

like the glass snowstorm in my chest
that your January dances
had shaken to blizzards.
My heart
inverted to a storm
forever ready to snow
unless
carelessly dropped, unless.

An even plows, officially sent,
flashed yellow eyes
and clinked their chains,
scraping ways through. Always

would be snow, tomorrow

would be snow. The dancing, drifting
and softly dropping days, and
your whitening whitening shoulder,
intending to carelessly turn
from anything not yet broken,
would only only

only be snow.

WHAT WHITE BECOMES

Little girl that walks on a world,
on a road, in a blizzard,
a globe inverted by a huge hand
somewhere, somewhere
is where you go.
How you carry your bag
drawn tightly closed and how snow
falls always on roads
and highways, swirling
every shape or shade
into purity and cold. Before
you become something old,
before your meltings are enough
that white becomes a cycle
not a wonder, and all quiet,
every melting noise
precipitates into memories
and wisdoms, and
unending tumbled whys,
you'll always be walking
on a world, on a road,
in a snowflake.

NATIVITY

The woman sways with donkey stride.
Bent over his shoulders,
she clutches his frozen mane
and her eyes become snow.
Her cheeks round and collapse.
She pants clouds. Heat rises in waves
again and again from her belly,
beading her forehead,
frosting ice into her hair.
Her mind hums along the edges
of each wrenching, each reprieve.

When the man lifts her and places her
tenderly into the stall,
she breathes pungent straw
and damp winter wool of sheep.
Animals chew hay. Their huge eyes
offering pity. A cow in the next stall
moans contentment as the woman
feels herself open, finally,
into flames. Her cry rises
with the bray of a donkey, then,

the cry of a child.
His hands, calloused and large
feel sweet against her cheeks
as Joseph whispers his warm breath
and news of a son against her ear.
Mary envelopes her baby.
His searching mouth nuzzles her breast.
Joseph yawns, waiting
for sleep to drift around them.
He blankets them with his robe.

As night wraps the stable
where the three of them
breathe into dreaming,
the animals sing stars
into darkening skies.
The animals sing omens.

INTO FROST AND FESTIVALS

So much snow
in sparkling mounds
that slope and cloud
around the drifted paths,
a snow night of silence,
landscape of prelude,
muffled purities and waiting.
Even those who've waited
snows or nights before
feel the question,
what could be beneath?

Forgotten seeds that split
their hulls, erupt crisp luminous
tendrils of wanting or needing
to be, swelling with random
permissions, ripening to quickness,
forgiving neglects, forgetting
not one thing, beneath
a steel sky
wrought iron trees
and street lights
casting yellows
against vanishing.

Black
can be felt. So much snow
wears it well at night, when
even white melts into grays,
our days have to diminish
as we trample them
into frost and festivals.
The ground freezes against
all journeys, hindered
by snow, and holds forgotten seeds
fast.

JANUARY

Day seems artificial,
this light,
January daylight,
when skies sag heavy with silver
beginning to tarnish,
the stream withdraws from flooding,
flexes and pulls itself
between banks
of frost and gray,
and greens so muted,
there is almost no yellow.
And all light-

light of breathing,
swelling lights of buds,
lights of how winter tilts-
all light
becomes florescent,
incandescent,
brittle light,
this January light,
from a sun
turning away.

A morning of purple and ice is held
within the circle of all that I see
from the bedroom window
just before another day
blushes its beginnings at the horizon
where a red circle of sun is crowning
and light is reaching long arms
across frozen, crystalline fields,
and I'm surprised by my joy
to be breathing still, and saddened
at how such a gorgeous world,
a planet too rare to be imagined,
can be idly forgotten as we hurry and fuss
through so many days, in our thoughtless rush
toward that moment of becoming
a dreaming, forgotten, unfeeling piece
of this dazzling earth,
all over again.

LOOKING BACK..

She may have been too much blizzard for him,
he may not have had the heart for winter,
he may have been the brightest dream
or blackest nightmare of her lifetime,
lost in drifts and somnambulent snow
and each slowly arriving tomorrow.

BESIDE THE WIDE RIVER

I never suspected it was the harp
how strings quivered
as we drove beside the Delaware
wanting

how a thousand rivers ran on car windows
and how water in the blood ran abreast
the river currents,

how wind beaten rain shivered
in the corners of pouring glass until
each pool blew away, and wipers
wipers wipers wipers wipers
temporary sweeps

each undone by clouds full of themselves,
but from arc to arc,
enough vision to stay on the road.
Every song of the ancient harp
rolled like waves, shivered

beside the Delaware. It rained
and rained and we wanted
the race across the muddy lot
to a restaurant table

and onion soup in thick brown bowls.
We blew across the steam, watched
the windows stream, and the river
full of itself, push against the banks.
We saw how wet a Sunday can be
when all of it rains
and our blood crested

beside the wide river.
When any ancient harp quivers,
we might drive again
beside the Delaware without
destinations, again swept
in Sunday grays, in flood time,

beside the Delaware
when rivers in our bodies surge
and a bittersweet harp is music

and our car windows rain
and the world rains

beside the wide river
as it curls above and beneath itself
and its water fills and empties, flows
away
but remains, water
in and beyond its sources and surface, water
that is the wide river.

APPRAISAL

Without doubt
the ocean is a jewel,
shimmering, changing
at will, and it will never
be set in anything
for permanence
or vanity, a jewel that rules
in blues and greens, salt
and gray, and foam flecked waves
roaring in, rolling out,
pulling forever before us
and after all of us, before
even the cooling of molten iron,
before the whirling of all matter
began to slow, before all
beginnings and after
the entirety of this planet
plays out its ages, after
eternity is only an infant,
and after all tomorrows
move into a now, the sea stays
for all time, beyond estimate
within its fathomless reign.

AT PERIMETERS OF SEAS

I almost remember
memories at the edges
dancing around deliberations
the mind reaches into the mood
but there is no brass ring
no matter how far I bend
how much I follow sighs
pounding along the hardest sand
that is always washed
and changed

at perimeters of seas
walking can be endless
crumbling rims of land
that only end at a beginning
but this is where I almost remember
air and just the wind are right for it
and even the gulls whose cree cree
is lost to horizons that don't exist
cree cree endlessly on
delivering voices like memories
that I can almost hold enough
at the perimeter of everywhere
on this journey that will not end.

BEACH MORNING

Single line of horizon
flaunting a false infinity,
slices straight across sky,
promising something beyond
its green gray end, forever
retreating from approach, seducing
voyages, remaining inscrutable,
the unreachable edge.

All morning eyes gaze to the line,
frame its existence within each
private misunderstanding, some of us
dream it to daydreams and beach haze,
some measure questions or troubles along
the definite line of its illusion, some
feel enough joy to diminish it, and some
put it all down in words as the task
recedes before her.

CASTING OFF

What would it have seemed
to Cro-Magnon or Neanderthal,
standing on the edge of a world, watching
water without end, moving and rolling,
rushing in, rushing away. How would they
understand an ocean under prehistoric skies?
Restless inside itself, like a roiling, discontented god,
at times so enraged it blackens sky and whips at winds,
rolling over land like a stampede of mammoths,
and then, just like a god, mysteriously calm, waves
softly kissing the sand, and at night across the surface,
blazed by a full moon, a glittering pathway
seeming to lead to the line of horizon,
to the end of all things.

This morning under the skies of my time,
I'm watching the same restless ocean.
A man crosses the beach and places his chair
securely at the rim of the sea. He holds a pole,
with a length of transparent line, baited
on its end with a piece of fish or meat, or
a lure of some fabricated shine on his hook.
He places himself at the edge of his world
with all his intentions, his casting off,
his morning efforts to catch
only a piece of it, just a small living part
of this vast and murmuring god.

THE RISING MOON

The rising moon over Atlantic horizon
makes a swath of glittering
we could walk across,
across the entire sea,
back to the moon,
to be home
again.

MOVEMENT IN SECTIONS

Reflecting is what makes a moon,
it could never own its light,
but can remember
flamboyancy,
learning it
and returning it.
When was a moon taught
to repeat across nothing
pale penmanship O's
through the large paragraphs
of stellar suicide?

What isn't a satellite of something?
Every motion in space selects a hub
and gleams of itself, or reflects
a separate burning.
Orbits are tossed like a woman's hair,
spinning through black,
tumbling and spiralling
around the knotted center.

Here and there
are windows to another black,
where light looks in
but cannot look out.
Tonight,
against the glass, the moon
presses a sectional smile, amused
and bored by pushing seas
and wet new lives
in gushes. Watch
in the thickly draped sky,

a pearly crescent and some coincidence.

FROM THE BALCONY BY THE ATLANTIC

The steely sky, offering a pale slice of moon,
carefully layers itself down from the heavens,
from blush gray to lavender gray, to iris gray,
to teal gray, green gray, to foamy lace edges
of breakers, to tan gray sand. And, when anything
chances to cross the gray layers, a sliver of fishing boat,
anything, three surfers gray riding in, anything,
a single kite tethered by the thread of a dream
to its diving suspended dance, whirling
across all grays with a flag of luminous tail,
as anything moves or slices through sacred gradations,
the grays and gray crossers mist in from the distance,
to brush against my eyes just as they notice,
on the farthest rim of horizon, a single shine
of a ship, gleaming between gray and teal gray,
so close to falling off the edge…and so now
it does fall, gone in a smudge of grays,
leaving me the desperate witness
trapped in a gaze.

DUSK BEYOND THE DUNES

The pale blue
holding a slice of faded moon,
colors itself carefully
to lavender gray,
to iris gray,
to gray, to teal gray,
to green gray,
to the lacy breakers edge.
Objects arrange themselves
within the grays:
a fishing boat, three surfers,
a single kite held only
by a child's dream
in its assigned, suspended dance,
with its luminous whirling tail.
In the distant horizon gray, just
between gray and teal gray,
a single, misted ship, so close
to falling off the edge,
and now it does, gone
in a smudge of grays,
with me
as witness.

WIND WALTZ

Storm clouds raise their instruments,
attentive to the rolling front,
directing distant soft thunders
to 3/4 time, the ballroom world
begins to darken.
Leaves swirl as branches bow
to the brazen winds, the dance
begins. Trees whirl and waltz
round and round until, finally,
the music softens, woodwind
breezes tiptoe delicate
to finale. The branches,
breathless, rest
against each other but
noisy leaves, closer to tree tops,
still flutter and rustle, eager
for another dance.

THUNDER SO DEAFENING

It stuns my ribs and
It rains and rains and rains
As if the sea intends our drowning
And has collected itself entirely into clouds
As if all the animals, plants and even the land
Are sentenced to be washed away
As if there is finally no redemption
For any life that does not swim
As if at last we are made to pay the price
For pouring our poisonous excess into the sea
As if our wars and marching have become too cruel
As if watery life, the oldest life, again
Will assume a natural dominion
As if the land itself is forced to take
One last breath and finally sink to the center
To the black depths under the waves
Where there is no light, no sound, no air
And not a single living tree.

SANDY

("…at 10 pm winds will range from 75-85 mph.")

When it reaches us, I feel the gods trying
to blow our home off the hillside and
I think of storms on Saturn, the raging winds on Pluto,
and the NOVA program describing how
light we see now is actually a planet or sun
already gone, maybe six billion years, swallowed
into a black hole, collapsed into a blue star, gone
into an alternate universe. Today,
before Sandy arrived, we couldn't see our sun
boiling in its own elements, radiating until
that predestined day it implodes into itself
or flares into super nova, erasing our world,
all blazing blue skies and ominous clouds,
every night lit city and us. Does it matter
that we finally understand how
some distant galaxy will, in millions
or billions of years, receive light waves
from our demise, watching them,
interpreting with their own evolving minds,
millennia after our milky way
has spilled away?

branches are brittly dead, snapping
at just a touch, or grey squirrel weight,
or passing deer, or the three of us
walking by. Boughs die
so much in these pines
as they jostle each other
in crowded green struggles
for sun.

In efforts to scrape
the itchy velvet of youth
from their antlers, young bucks
strip bark from slender trunks,
bend saplings to ruin.

Through fragrant tree destructions
the deer traffic moves,
spotted fawns to sleek doe
to magnificent racks to battles
to matings to grazings

to one licensed rifle
deep
in the evergreen cover.

DEER VISITS

Coming through November fallen leaves,
steps sound larger than we want to hear,
alone in a state forest, alone
in a campground, at night. But when
we recognize the slender face, large ears,
amazing eyes, when we see
a magical deer approach us, we are happy,
eager to talk to her, and she is near enough,
watching us, smelling the air, moving her ears
at my invitations, my conversation all my own.

We call her our deer, and she visits often,
walking through our campsite again and again,
stopping each time, comfortable with us,
curious, maybe happy to see us we wish but
even if there is a notion of beauty
or magic anywhere in deer thought,
I'm not so sure we
would seem either.

HORIZON

From my 6th floor office window,
I gaze at the line of mountain and rooftops
that forms the horizon and think
about having been alive
for more than sixty years, attended
memorials and funerals for friends
I believed would always be with me,
as I imagined I would always
be with them, watching the horizon
shimmer as I blink against the tears
that want to come. I keep staring
at the distance, and hearing
the panting, slavering hound of mortality
closing the distance behind me, and
I imagine the small moment when
my father's eager cell passed through
the membrane of my mother's cell, when
immediately, I dropped out of eternity
to flash wildly into flesh, and the time,
my time, began to tick itself down
toward my horizon
and its vanishing point.

MONSIGNOR MANTIS

Mantis preying
posing mechanical
on a knobby twig,
mandibles moving,
devoutly snatching,
chewing,
reverently grinding life
to buzzless juices,
swallowed into
hallowed places.
Praying mantis,
monster face,
unblinking
faceted
eyes.

SPRUCE MUSIC

The music beneath spruce

winds around ivy vines,
where dew coated webs,
backlit by early sun,
are redwood bracelets,
and redwood sighs
tumble over themselves,
somersaulting with eucalyptus,
angels, other minor souls.

In the mind of its own time

this moment holds itself
beyond ink or inclinations,
seduction is accomplished
with intentions; one red deer
near the white pines
is convinced to follow
her forehead all the way
to a clearing.

Only a moment loved enough

will be embraced,
held between linen,
memorized to novelty,
caressed into tenderness,
embossed onto bond,
like the music beneath spruce
that winds around ivy vines
with other minor souls.

THE EAGLE RIDE

The sky unfurls a blue
that needs no stars
this 4th of July weekend.
I shift down to climb the hill, pedaling slowly,
my mind drifting with summer perfumes
when I see him in the alfalfa field,
starting to run, stretching wings, lifting
above the tree rows, rising into the air,
an American eagle.
His white head and tail feathers
are unmistakable. He suspends himself
like a dream in the radiant blue.
We stop our bikes just to watch him.
I've never seen an eagle in the wild!
We say it together, mirrored in each others'
huge eyes. The eagle circles, an amazement,
free in air that everyone breathes,
above a planet that everyone shares,
hovering forever, belonging
to no one, his meaning more
than what is assigned.

SPIRIT BEARS

Long ago, the story goes, the world was covered in ice and snow. One day, the raven, the creator of the world, came down from heaven and turned the world green, as it is today. But as a reminder of the time when all was white, the raven went among the bears and turned every tenth one the color of snow. The raven decreed that the white bear would live forever in peace. – Legend of the Spirit Bear

In the book about our singular God, He is credited
with starting all of it and with making one form of life
called man to look like Him, and giving man dominion
over all, that's what's written in the book about our singular God.

People of other gods, in their soft confusions,
stare with wonder as trees fall, water is poisoned,
animals slaughtered and not used for food,
not used at all. Some people with different gods,
don't see clear division between their living
and all other life.

On a northern Canadian coast a few hundred white bears
called "spirit bears" still exist. They are the last
of the white bears held sacred by those
following different gods. In the books of their gods,
the bears were made white to remind how ice
once covered all the land until the great spirit
made it green again. As reminders from god,
the spirit bears are not to be harmed.

But homes, offices, staircases, hallways, conference tables,
entertainment centers, paper plates, cardboard boxes,
movie posters, backyard decks, tearing down buildings,
building new buildings, man is needing more trees,
needing the trees in the home of the spirit bears.
It becomes a battle to protect the bears and their home.

The last place of these few hundred magic bears,
the only remaining spirit bears, is a lush, northern
rainforest on Princess Royal Island,
where the trees are older than history,
older even than the book of our singular God,
the One said to have given this dominion,
this damned dominion, over anything in the way.

Kathleen Moser lives in New Tripoli, Pennsylvania with her husband. She spent years working as a medical editor, raising two children, and recovering from childhood abuse. Much of her early successes in publication were in poetry journals until she had to withdraw from all of that to deal with flashbacks and healing. She has never stopped writing and finally, at the urging of her husband, she has decided to put the books out there. She and her husband David have 3 grandchildren. Life is a blessing.